ZENSHO W. KOPP

The radiating clarity of the mind

The radiating sun of absolute consciousness, deep within our hearts, is the eternal presence of the divine within us. Those who do not know this inner chamber at the deepest base of our being have missed out on life's essence.

Nothing should be more important in our lives than to recognise this, our birthless and deathless true essence.

All people are seeking absolute bliss without actually knowing that they are seeking it.

Yet, when your true self, which is pure, divine bliss, breaks free within you, you recognise that everything you previously took to be happiness was just illusion.

The original nature of the own mind is free from the thought processes of dualistic perception. The intellect neither fixates nor objectifies sense objects. Everything is perceived as a completely empty expanse.

In the experience of enlightenment of the mind, detached from everything, this boundless expanse of the mind reveals itself as the timeless equality of all being.

Your suffering comes from seeking for a higher state of being, fulfilment in life and inner peace in the external world of objects.

As long as you are still convinced you can find something externally that can offer you a greater sense of being and permanent satisfaction, you remain dependent on external factors as a victim of your illusions.

Nothing is important in the face of the presence of death. Death is absolute reality and can come at any time without warning.

It is therefore a great tragedy to waste one's life in mindless routine and indifferent ignorance, caught in a myriad of trivialities.

Undistractedness is the noble path of all buddhas of the past, present and future.

Therefore, abide everywhere and at all times, no matter where you are and what you are doing, in awareness of the immediate presence of your unchanging, true self.

The greatest barrier to perceiving our true essence is the conviction that we already know who we really are.

Everything you believe yourself to be is nothing more than empty, dead concepts. These beliefs are no true understanding but just self-deception.

People have many pretexts why they do not take time to delve into the truth of life and death. Their whole life passes by in indifferent ignorance, filled with illusions and vanities.

In the end, at the moment of death, they are caught in their belief in the absolute reality of the ego and the glorification of their thoughts in samsara, the existence cycle of birth and death.

All life is an inexplicable, wonderful mystery. What life and consciousness truly are, is beyond all explanation and definition. Everything one could say about them would miss the point.

Therefore, why try to explain the beauty of a flower?

Those who live by the truth of Zen need not follow any external rules. They live their free, unbound lives completely naturally, in unison with heaven and earth. In the midst of the hustle and bustle of the world, they constantly abide in attentive clarity and imperturbability of the mind.

This is fire lotus Zen, the lotus that does not burn in the fire of samsara.

Lingering on foregone experiences and repeatedly recalling them is a complete waste of time.

The past is irrevocably gone and mourning after pleasant moments you once experienced only leads to a state of yearning and thus suffering.

However, in constant awareness of the absolute, present moment, we let go of the past and find peace within us.

Achievement, esteem and possessions cannot bestow us with lasting happiness and fulfilment. They are all impermanent, like bubbles of air in empty space.

True happiness can only be found in the ever-lasting – in eternal being, which reveals itself in the absolute presence of Here and Now.

True devotion and worship of the divine are much more than wallowing in pleasant feelings and the commonly held, dualistic belief in a God who exists only in one's thoughts.

Instead, they are a silent, mysterious movement of the heart, emanating from a higher understanding of the inner presence of the divine.

The ultimate goal of all spiritual paths is to utterly forget ourselves and all things by turning to our divine origin.

This means immersing ourselves in the innermost core of our hearts and dissolving into the boundless light of absolute consciousness.

It is a homecoming to the original state of our true essence.

In Zen meditation it makes no difference whether thoughts arise or not. It is important that we do not follow them, becoming diverted or that we try to forcefully suppress them.

In intentionless awareness of mind, simply let the thoughts come and go without taking heed of them. This is how you recognise them in their empty nature and your meditation takes place of its own accord.

A person's state of spiritual unknowing is as great as the conditioned and thus limited state of their thinking.

It is equivolent to their attachment to the interwoven memories of their dead past. Identifying with your memories causes attachment and this is the remnants of foregone experiences that have etched themselves in your consciousness.

You will only know what the truth is when you yourself dive into the ocean of wisdom, into the boundless expanse of the One Mind.

Once you have transcended the boundaries of your intellect this way, you rise up into bound-lessness.

What is your true self? What is your true self beyond birth and death? As long as you do not seek to fathom this, your whole life – regardless of what you have achieved – is completely meaningless and without value.

Even if you know everything about religion and philosophy, when the moment of death arrives, it is of no value to you and you will still be attached to the cycle of birth and death.

Through a profound understanding of the illusory
and dream-like nature of life and the imper-
manence of all things we achieve a liberating,
inner lightness.

We experience our life with more awareness
and meaning, and our relationships become more
sincere.

By believing in the dream you take to be life, you remain chained to the cycle of existence of birth and death. However, you have the possibility to stop dreaming and wake up.

When you have achieved this awakened, clear state of being of all-uniting vastness, you neither see an external world, nor a mind within. Everything blossoms in the enlightened void of the One Mind.

When you experience boundless enlightenment, you cease to exist, for your assumed personality dissolves away completely.

In this moment of grace, your true essence radiates as pure, deathless being, brighter than a thousand suns.

Spontaneous liberation by experiencing your original essence takes place by abiding without any intentions in naturally occurring timeless consciousness, pure thusness, just as it is, in a clear state of boundless vastness.

Retaining this open clarity of mind in all things is the prerequisite to experiencing your original buddha-nature.

Water waves cannot exist without water itself. Likewise, all beings appear solely in the open vastness of the mind, without ever being separated from it. Meditation brings us into contact with our true self, which by experiencing this all-embracing wholeness of being, is completely one with everything.

This experience of consubstantiality is the real basis of all true compassion.

Human life is extremely valuable, for it is a wonderful opportunity for realising our immortal, true essence.

Therefore, turn your awareness inwards and recognise your birthless and deathless true self before the curtain on the stage of life and death for ever falls.

Buddhahood is nowhere to be found in the world. You can only achieve consummate enlightenment by recognising your true, original essence.

Great enlightenment means directly recognising your radiating own mind and experiencing that your own true essence is indestructible and originally free from birth and death.

Complete liberation from all concepts and attachments and dissolving into the fullness of divine
being are one, sole experience and take place in
the same instant.

Now-Here, this instant, right there where you are,
the reality of your birthless and deathless true
essence reveals itself. Therefore, immerse yourself
in it right now!

As long as you still try to act in a way so as to please others, you will always be someone other than you really are.

As the sum of your concepts, you are not yourself but are bound to the conditioned reactions of those around you.

Our devotion to the divine reaches its peak in a radical self-renunciation at the moment of mystical death.

In the search for divine essence, the seeker himself must lose himself. As paradox as it may sound, we can only experience our true self when there is no longer anyone there who can experience it.

All that exists is fundamentally empty and only-mind. There is no thinker behind the thoughts, whose rapid and complex succession gives the impression of a continuous consciousness.

Thoughts arise from the void and sink once again into the void.

平安清

All difficulties arise solely from discriminating thought. When thoughts cease, all difficulties vanish and the original cheerfulness of the mind reveals itself as your true nature.

True peace is when you are free from the compulsion of discriminating thinking. When you achieve this inner peace, you are at peace everywhere.

In their essence, the One Mind and your own mind are one and the same reality. Thus, perceiving the nature of your own mind means perceiving the true nature of the all-embracing wholeness of being.

When you perceive the mind, the mind is Buddha. Yet when you do not perceive it, it is the ego-delusion. Buddha is real, the ego-delusion is illusion.

Do not make yourself a slave of human senti-
ment. The consciousness of all the buddhas takes
place when all habitual thinking and feeling cease.

In a moment of crystal-clear awareness without
discrimination, great wisdom appears.

When you are free from affection and rejection, you are free from your desires, and discriminating thoughts become silent of their own accord.

Spiritual serenity of non-discriminating clarity of the mind frees you from worldly entanglement and your mind abides unwaveringly in the peace of the self.

The cheerful, serene reflection of the mind is an intentionless, crystal-clear self-awareness in the peaceful silence of non-thinking.

This crystal-clear self-awareness, which exists without the need for thoughts, and thus neither blocks nor fabricates anything, is the pure state of the mind. It is the original, enlightened heart-consciousness of all buddhas.

By nature, the mind itself is completely open and empty. Thus, there is nothing you can meditate on. So abide without distraction in the boundless expanse of non-meditation.

In this natural, intentionless consciousness state, a profound and essential dimension of existence reveals itself, in which you experience the true nature of your mind.

If you wish to experience your true essence, it is essential that you leave all deceptions behind you.

However, the thought of having left all deceptions behind you is the first deception you have to rid yourself of.

When erroneous thoughts vanish, the original mind appears of its own accord.

It is as though you are polishing a mirror; when you have wiped away the dust, everything is transparent through and through, and beginning-less, radiating clarity appears of its own accord.

Your true essence is of original purity and clarity. It is a timeless, spontaneous present state of pure being and consummate awareness.

When your consciousness is completely clear and detached and without any point of reference, you transcend your pseudo-identity caused by your ego-delusion and experience yourself as the boundless expanse of the mind.

Allow your consciousness to open into the absolute presence of Now in the boundless expanse of the mind.

Without rejecting or welcoming thoughts, recognise that they are the fundamental, dynamic energy of the mind and abide relaxed, in cheerful reflection of the mind.

Worries and fears are a pointless burden for our mind and prevent us from experiencing our divine nature. When ruminating thoughts arise, great confusion follows, and thus all problems.

Therefore, Zen says: liberate your mind from every-thing and you shall abide in cloudless, radiating clarity.

Cleanse your mind from dualistic thinking, for you are absolute, pure awareness, free from all attachments. Only your discriminating ego-thinking causes the illusion.

In an instant, the wise one slices through the roots of ignorance with the sword of perception and thus achieves consummate liberation.

You identify yourself with your mortal body because you have lost contact with your true self, which knows no death.

Forget yourself and, filled with trust, give yourself to divine being. Then you no longer need fear death, quite the opposite in fact.

Whoever has liberated themselves from all identifications will be united with the radiating light of the mind in the process of death.

The truth is that our true self, as the eternal, timeless reality of our true essence, was never born and will never die.

Our birth is not the beginning of life since our true essence exists before our birth, and this means: we are life. And since our true essence is already there before birth, it will also be there after death.

You constantly experience nothing other than the world that pertains to your state of consciousness, for the world you experience is a reflection of your own projections.

You create your own world. This means that when your consciousness is in a state of grasping and rejecting, you are trapped in your own projections.

The highest truth only reveals itself to you when every dualistic perspective is shattered with the sharp sword of non-discriminating wisdom.

When you clear your mind through the power of concentrated awareness so that you melt with the divine essence in your innermost self, the flower of the One Mind will suddenly blossom within you.

The awakened one, who has completely eradicated the delusion of an ego, becomes a mirror in which each person can perceive their divine image.

The sole, divine self is the centre point of an awakened person, whose mysterious energy field brings to life an inkling within us of inner oneness.

Since your true essence is formless, it cannot be grasped, for it is beyond all sensory and intellectual perception.

However, without knowledge, the highest knowledge of an awakened consciousness understands all things and perceives all things in their essential reality.

If the mind would not project any external phenomena, there would be no illusion of time passing. The space-time illusion is a result of the constantly changing projections of the mind.

When you recognise this, you liberate yourself from your attachment to a seemingly real, objective world and you no longer entangle yourself in reactions to your own projections.

Everything you experience is just phenomena of your own mind and thus the mind itself.

Everything – body, mind and world – is merely a game of the mind in which and through which all things manifest themselves, transform and vanish once more, like in a dream.

Buddha means the awakened one. Stop your dreaming and you are Buddha.

Your state of mind at the moment of death is of vital importance. Your mental formations at the end of your life lead, as karmic driving forces, to the next world-experience, which is a mirror of these karmic forces.

For this reason, it is very important at the moment of death to abide in a clear, tranquil state of mind, free from identifications and attachments.

In death, your own world dies with you. Equally, in birth, your own world is born. Ultimately, this means that you were not born into a world in space and time that existed before you and consequently, when you die, you will not leave any world behind you.

In a state of inner tranquillity of mind, all concepts of the ego-forming interwoven memory of your dead past vanish into the radiating clarity of the mind. This is the true Zen way to liberation.

When all thinking suddenly ceases, you experience the state of pure awareness and will perceive your brightly shining true essence in its profoundest depths.

The splendour of divine being is no unreachable, far-off, transcendental dimension, for it is now, here, right where you currently are.

Reality reveals itself this instant, right here. Immerse yourself completely in this instant! This is the direct Zen way of instantaneously grasping reality just as it is.

The realisation of pure self-awareness dissolves all discriminating thoughts into the void and allows your buddha-nature to shine forth.

When the divine light in the soul becomes aflame, the divineness of the world and all life is recognised and accomplished.

Whoever has awakened to the true nature of the mind is beyond birth and death so that the question of "to be or not to be" has lost its meaning for them.

This person, rooted in the timeless reality of the Tao, becomes a revelation of the Tao in the midst of the world and attains immortality beyond death.

平安清

Life passes by as quickly as a leaf, blown past the window on the autumn wind.

In view of this undeniable fact, each person should reconsider their situation in life. They should become aware of the insignificance of their worldly strivings and desires in the light of their own, inevitable mortality.

In Buddhism, the great void, "Shunyata," is the perfection of the fullness of divine nothingness.

It is absolute reality, in which there is neither scarcity nor abundance, but just an eternal, blissful silence, in which all action comes to rest.

Everything that the mind and the senses can perceive is the deception of the mind and thus illusion.

Reality lies beyond the perceivable and is completely free from ego-notion and duality. It is the innermost essence of everything, the sole, eternal self.

Your true self is not dependent on anything, it relies on nothing that is separate from itself, for it has no other root besides itself because there is nothing else besides it.

All plurality is illusion. There is just a sole essence, the One Mind, beside which nothing else exists. It is the sole reality at the deepest base of all beings and things.

When your mind is completely present and clear in a state of inner tranquillity, you become aware of your true, immortal essence, which is present Now-Here in timeless eternity.

True prayer is when you abide without intentions in this silent clarity of mind, in which you immerse yourself devotedly in a state in which there is absolutely no distinction from highest reality.

There is no gradual enlightenment, instead just a sudden awakening to the reality of our birthless and deathless true being.

The moment you experience great enlightenment is like the blossoming of the lotus flower. It is just like the sudden awakening of a dreamer.

Your true, undying self is the radiating light of the mind, which dissolves all darkness and deception.

The moment you awaken, the clouds of discriminating thought disappear and the mind radiates into the boundless expanse and the void. In this experience, the entire universe rotates around itself and a completely different realm of being appears.

In truth, nothing exists beyond inseparable, absolute consciousness, which is experienced in the timeless eternity of Now as pure awareness.

There is neither birth nor death, attachment nor liberation, just the uniform, all-pervading reality of the One Mind, which is your primal, true essence.

The perpetual presence of the true, divine self within you means that in mystical immersion, it can become your own living experience.

It is essential to have an unshakeable belief in the original purity of the mind.

In its unrestrictedness it fills the entire universe, eternally shining.

Highest spiritual realisation is an abandonment of one's own ego in utter devotion to unchanging, highest reality.

Only when the delusion of an ego has been completely wiped out does the light of your true divine self reveal itself in your heart. It is like when the sun burst out in its radiating light following a solar eclipse.

Those who awaken to the birthless and deathless reality of their true self in the enlightenment experience, witness themselves as unborn and un-dying and as eternity itself.

They have broken through the barrier of birth and death and have returned to the origin of all being, to the eternal source of all life.

Impressum

First edition 2021

Original title "Die strahlende Klarheit des Geistes",
published by Spirit Rainbow Verlag, Aachen, Germany 2021

Original idea and design: Verena Kopp

Image editing: Reinhard Zanella

Translation: John Kitching

Typesetting: Reinhard Zanella

Cover design: Michel Schmidt

Back cover photo: Axel Jung

© 2023 Zensho W. Kopp

Production and publishing:

BoD - Books on Demand, Norderstedt

ISBN: 9783752689518

Zensho W. Kopp, born 1938, is one of the most significant spiritual masters of our present times and teaches a contemporary path to spiritual realisation. The internationally renowned author of numerous Zen books and audio books instructs a large community of students and directs the Zen Center Tao Chan in Wiesbaden, Germany.

Tao Chan Zentrum e.V., Non-profit society, Wiesbaden.
More info at: **www.tao-chan.org**

Twice a month, the Zen Center Tao Chan organises an online Zen-evening with a talk by Zen Master Zensho W. Kopp, where guests are welcome to attend. There is also the possibility to ask Zen Master Zensho questions.

Register here for the online evening:
www.tao-chan.org/events/events-zen-night.html

Zen Center Tao Chan
www.youtube.com/@zencentertaochan

Subscribe here for free short talks by Zen Master Zensho W. Kopp:
www.youtube.com/@zencentertaochan/shorts

Facebook site for the Zen Center Tao Chan
www.facebook.com/zencentertaochan

Further books by Zensho W. Kopp

also available as **eBook** in ePUB and Kindle format

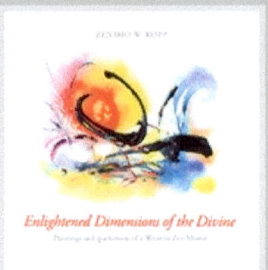

Modern ZEN-ART, Watercolours and sayings of a Western Zen Master.
124 pages, 23,50 €

Enlightened Dimensions of the Divine, Paintings and quotations of a Western Zen Master
140 pages, 10,50 €

The Flame of Awareness
124 pages

Living in inner fullness
116 pages, 9,80 €

The power of inner quietude
104 pages, 9,80 €

The radiating clarity of the mind
136 pages

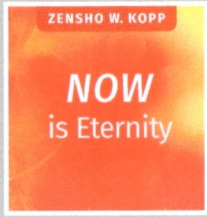

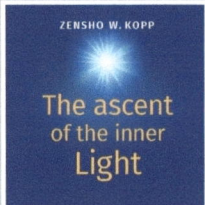

Now is Eternity
114 pages, 9,80 €

The ascent of the inner Light
114 pages

The immortality of the true self
104 pages

The mystery of true self-perception
124 pages

Further books by Zensho W. Kopp
also available as **eBook** in ePUB and Kindle format

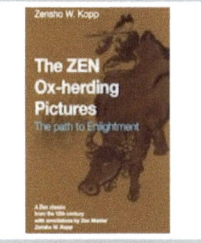

The ZEN Ox-herding Pictures
The path to Enlightment
212 pages, 9,95 €

True Life Through Zen
Spiritual self-realisation in daily life
140 pages, 11,50 €

Awakening to Your True Self
The Zen way of all-embracing mysticism
140 pages, 11,99 €

Lao-tse Tao Te King
The book of Tao and spiritual force
120 pages, 7,95 €

All publications by Zensho can be found and purchased here:
www.tao-chan.org/zen-master-zensho/books.html

Further books by Zensho W. Kopp

also available as **eBook** in ePUB and Kindle format

**The Direct Zen-Way
to Liberation**
212 pages, 9,95 €

ZEN in daily life
187 pages

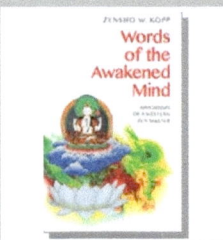

**Words of the
Awakened Mind**
140 pages, 9,95 €

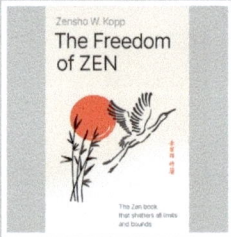

The Freedom of ZEN
216 pages

Audio books by Zensho W. Kopp

True life through ZEN
Read by Christopher Kent
Audiobook (CD), MP3 down-
load, Audible Audiobook
8,95 €

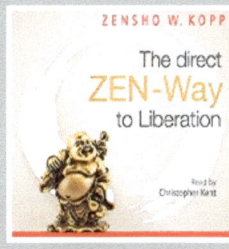

**The direct ZEN-WAY
to Liberation**
Read by Christopher Kent
Audiobook (CD), MP3 down-
load, Audible Audiobook
9,95 €

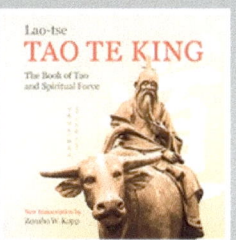

Lao-Tse Tao te King
Read by Christopher Kent
Audiobook (CD), MP3 down-
load, Audible Audiobook
10,95 €

**Awakening to your
True Self**
Read by Jonathan Lloyd
Audiobook (CD), MP3 down-
load, Audible Audiobook
10,95 €

All publications by Zensho can be found and purchased here:
www.tao-chan.org/zen-master-zensho/audiobooks.html

Photo credits

123rf

1. Nikolay Mossolaynen – Image nr. 112957816
2. Maryna Sokolyan – Image nr. 131949281
3. Alexey Burmakin – Image nr. 35587376
4. mpmpya – Image nr. 43815327
5. mpmpya – Image nr. 43815385
6. mpmpya – Image nr. 43815430
7. mpmpya – Image nr. 46657210
8. mpmpya – Image nr. 46657429
9. Kseniia Pasynkova – Image nr. 51289110
10. zzvet – Image nr. 57217736
11. rie0914 – Image nr. 63151440
12. zenina – Image nr. 67562976
13. seita – Image nr. 68300625
14. rie0914 – Image nr. 77105723
15. Masaaki Abe – Image nr. 80369415
16. Tetiana Syrytsyna – Image nr. 81759724
17. matriyoshka – Image nr. 86249534
18. Maksim Borzdov – Image nr. 99415555

AdobeStock

1. leshabu – Image nr. 31349372
2. Siam Vector – Image nr. 355259703

istockphoto

1. hpkalyani – Image nr. 165749758
2. yangzai – Image nr. 469765051
3. Elinalee – Image nr. 684450764
4. sarun rodjanaudomwuttikul – Image nr. 964955554

shutterstock

1. Siam Vector – Image nr. 1092842255
2. Yumeee – Image nr. 1137067043
3. Gluiki – Image nr. 1169834995
4. Phoebe Yu – Image nr. 1247696755
5. Nezabudkina – Image nr. 430915579
6. Yumeee – Image nr. 758755327